KT-226-116

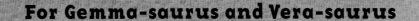

For Gemma-saurus and Vera-saurus

**The Authors and Publishers would like
to thank Dr Angela Milner, Deputy Keeper of Palaeontology
at the Natural History Museum, London for her help and advice.**

Dino-Dinners copyright © Frances Lincoln Limited 2006
Text and illustrations copyright © Mick Manning and Brita Granström 2006

First published in Great Britain in 2006 by
Frances Lincoln Children's Books, 4 Torriano Mews,
Torriano Avenue, London NW5 2RZ
www.franceslincoln.com

First paperback edition published in 2006.

All rights reserved.
No part of this publication may be reproduced,
stored in a retrieval system, or transmitted, in any form, or by any means,
electrical, mechanical, photocopying, recording or otherwise without
the prior written permission of the publisher or a licence permitting restricted copying.
In the United Kingdom such licences are issued by the Copyright Licensing Agency,
90 Tottenham Court Road, London W1P 9HE.

British Library Cataloguing in Publication Data available on request

ISBN 10: 1-84507-689-3
ISBN 13: 978-1-84507-689-4

The illustrations have been done in watercolour and pencil.

Printed in China
3 5 7 9 8 6 4 2

Visit Mick and Brita at www.mickandbrita.com

5679
D. CREW

MICK MANNING

grew up in Haworth, West Yorkshire. He studied Illustration
at the Royal College of Art in London.

BRITA GRANSTRÖM

grew up on a farm in Sweden. She studied Illustration
at Konstfack in Stockholm.

Mick and Brita were recently featured
on the BBC Blue Peter Awards 2005. Their distinctive books
have won many prizes over the years, including The Smarties Silver Prize,
The TES Award and The English Association Award. Brita won
the prestigious Oppenheim Toy Portfolio Platinum award in the USA
for *Does a Cow say Boo?* with Judy Hindley. Mick and Brita's
books with Frances Lincoln include *Yuck!* and *Snap!*
and the English Award-nominated *Fly on the Wall*
history series.

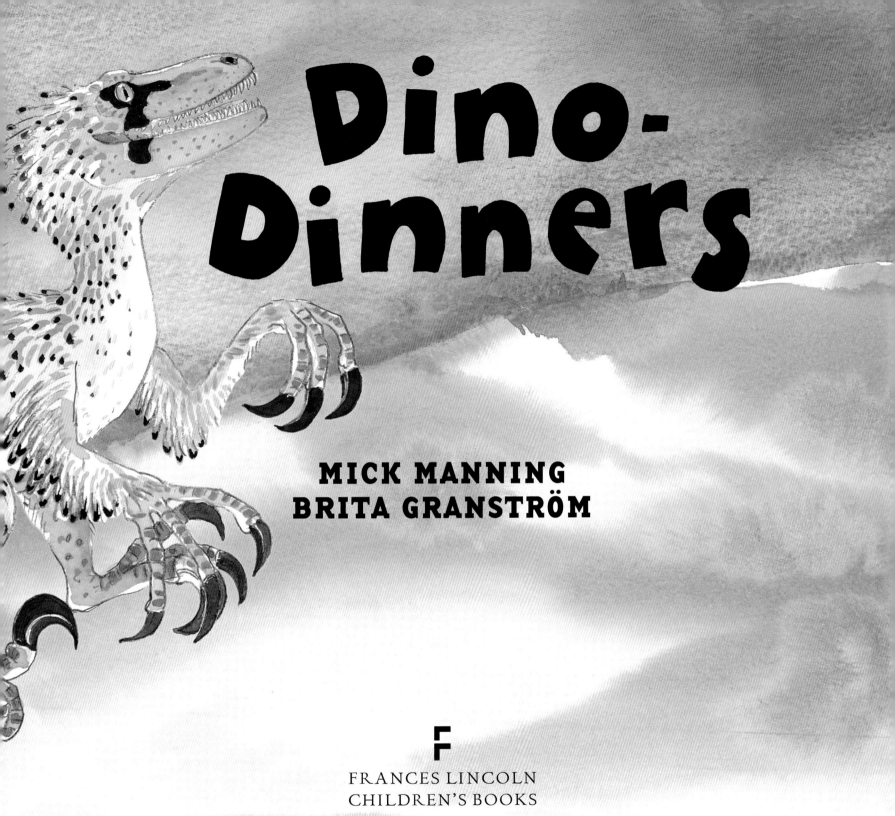

Dino-Dinners

MICK MANNING
BRITA GRANSTRÖM

F

FRANCES LINCOLN
CHILDREN'S BOOKS

In association with the
Natural History Museum, London

Oviraptor

I eat cones, shellfish and nuts –

cracking eggs can be tasty too.

Best of all, a fat crunchy beetle,

snatched from the top

of a dinosaur poo.

Oviraptor

(Oh-vee-rap-tor)
* Lived 85 – 75 million years ago
* Nose to tail: 1.8 metres
* Omnivore

Oviraptor stood on two legs and was a fast emu-sized dinosaur.

Nobody is sure what *Oviraptor* ate but it was probably omnivorous, eating both plants and meat.

Using its strong beak, it could easily have crushed nuts, bones, insects, eggs and shellfish.

Euoplocephalus

(You-op-loh-keff-ah-lus)
* Lived 74 – 71 million years ago
* Nose to tail: up to 7 metres
* Herbivore

Euoplocephalus' heavy clubbed tail could inflict broken bones on predators. No predator wants to risk that. A serious injury means 'game over'.

Euoplocephalus' tail weighed up to 30 kilos. Its tailbones were strengthened to swing this heavy weight.

It was armoured like a tank and probably crouched low, if attacked, to stop a predator trying to flip it over on to its back.

Euoplocephalus

Here I come!

Trundling through the woodland plants,

I'm always on the look-out

for danger as I munch.

Armoured legs, armoured body, armoured face,

clubbed tail a-swinging – just in case.

Mind out!

Tyrannosaurus rex

(Tie-ran-oh-sore-us rex)

* Lived 67– 65 million years ago
* Nose to tail: 12 metres
* Carnivore

Tyrannosaurus rex's crushing bite and keen sense of smell meant that it could feed on the largest herbivores – alive or dead!

Tyrannosaurus nestlings would have been covered in downy fluff to keep them warm.

Tyrannosaurus rex

I like sick and injured dinos,

or dead dinos that really pong!

I'm a giant with a giant's appetite

and I love rotten meat –

it doesn't put up a fight!

Triceratops

(Try-ker-ah-tops)
* Lived 67–65 million years ago
* Nose to tail: 9 metres
* Herbivore

Teeth-marks that match *Tyrannosaurus rex* teeth have been found in the fossil bones of *Triceratops*.

Triceratops would have charged like a modern rhino.

Triceratops

I eat plants – but be warned!

I'll charge anyone, anytime!

My horns have six tons of muscle

and bone behind them.

I am a very dangerous veggie.

You'll soon see,

if you ever mess with me!

Edmontosaurus

I am one of a crowd – a herd that trumpets and grunts to each other. My jaws and cheeks help my teeth grind, grate and crush: turning every delicious mouthful of my veggie dino-dinner into mush.

Edmontosaurus

(Ed-mont-oh-sore-us)
* Lived 76–67 million years ago
* Nose to tail: up to 13 metres
* Herbivore

Edmontosaurus was a hadrosaur living in herds in open plains and woodlands.

Its jaws moved in a unique sideways chewing movement making its teeth act like a cheese grater.

Some hadrosaurs had bony crests to recognise others of their own kind. Some called to each other using large 'trumpet' chambers in their heads.

Velociraptor

(Vel-oss-ee-rap-tor)

* Lived 80–73 million years ago
* Nose to tail: 1.8 metres
* Carnivore

Velociraptor was a pack hunter like modern wolves.

Velociraptor had feathers to keep warm. Flapping feathered arms may also have helped it balance.

A *Velociraptor* and a *Protoceratops* were found fossilized together! They died fighting each other and were covered with blowing sand.

Huge toe claws helped it climb up on to the backs of large prey.

Velociraptor

Big or small, there's no escape once my gang give chase. We sprint... and leap,

climbing leathery mountains of dino flesh with the huge claws on our feet.

Then comes our favourite part –

EAT! EAT! EAT!

Coelophysis

(Seel-oh-fie-sis)

* Lived 225 – 220 million years ago
* Nose to tail: 3 metres
* Carnivore

Coelophysis lived early in the age of dinosaurs.

Fossilised Coelophysis have been found with chewed-up young in their stomachs.

They may well have been under stress from starvation and drought, but this still makes them dino-cannibals.

Coelophysis

We prowl the landscape, hunting for prey. When times get hard we'll eat our own kind if they get in our way.

Any bite-size version of ourselves will do –
a meaty niece, a crunchy nephew...

Iguanodon

Pond plants are a tasty dino-dinner for us.
We browse slowly and quietly,
munching as we move.
Then comes the noisy part –
the more we eat,
the more we fart!

Iguanodon

(Ig-wha-noh-don)

* Lived 130 – 115 million years ago
* Nose to tail: up to 10 metres
* Herbivore

Iguanodon used the 'little finger' on each hand to grip and pull leafy stems to its mouth.

All that plant food made *Iguanodon's* large stomach fizz up like a bottle of pop, producing a lot of gas!

Iguanodon's huge thumb spike was its only defence against predators like *Baryonyx*.

Baryonyx

Fresh fish are my favourite.

I swipe them with my hooked claws

and swallow them one at a time:

head, fins and scales –

all coated in slippery slime!

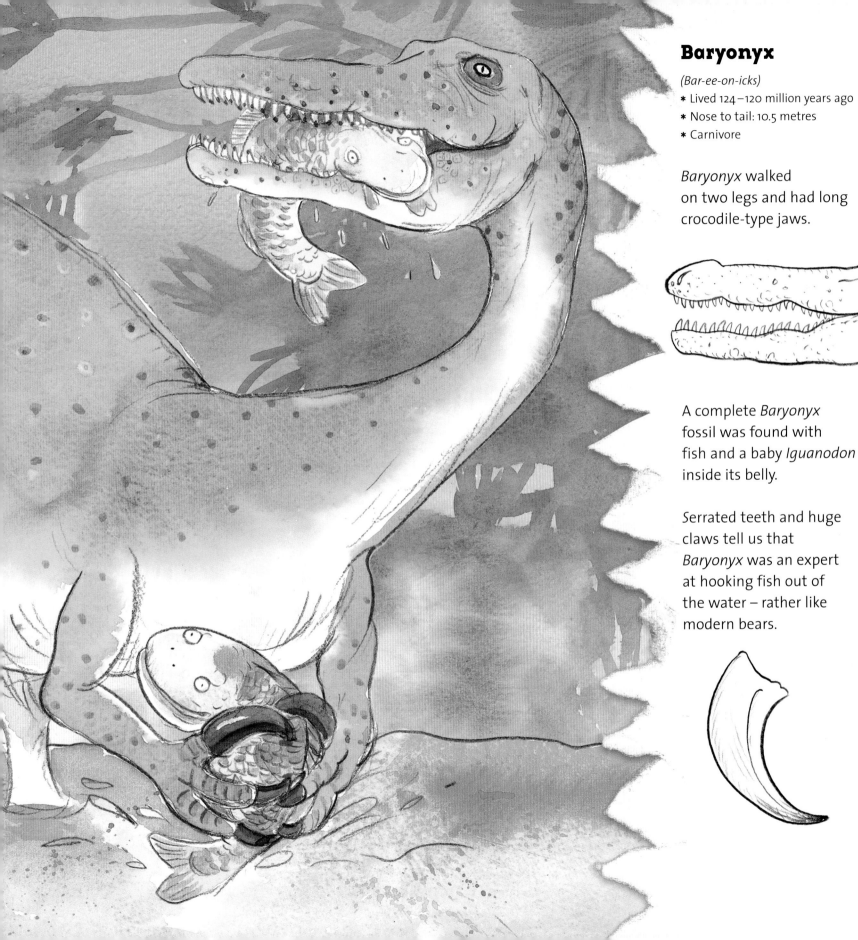

Baryonyx

(Bar-ee-on-icks)

* Lived 124–120 million years ago
* Nose to tail: 10.5 metres
* Carnivore

Baryonyx walked on two legs and had long crocodile-type jaws.

A complete *Baryonyx* fossil was found with fish and a baby *Iguanodon* inside its belly.

Serrated teeth and huge claws tell us that *Baryonyx* was an expert at hooking fish out of the water – rather like modern bears.

Brachiosaurus

(Brak-ee-oh-sore-us)
* Lived 155 – 140 million years ago
* Nose to tail: up to 25 metres
* Herbivore

Brachiosaurus and some other plant-eaters swallowed small pebbles called gastroliths to help digest the plants they ate.

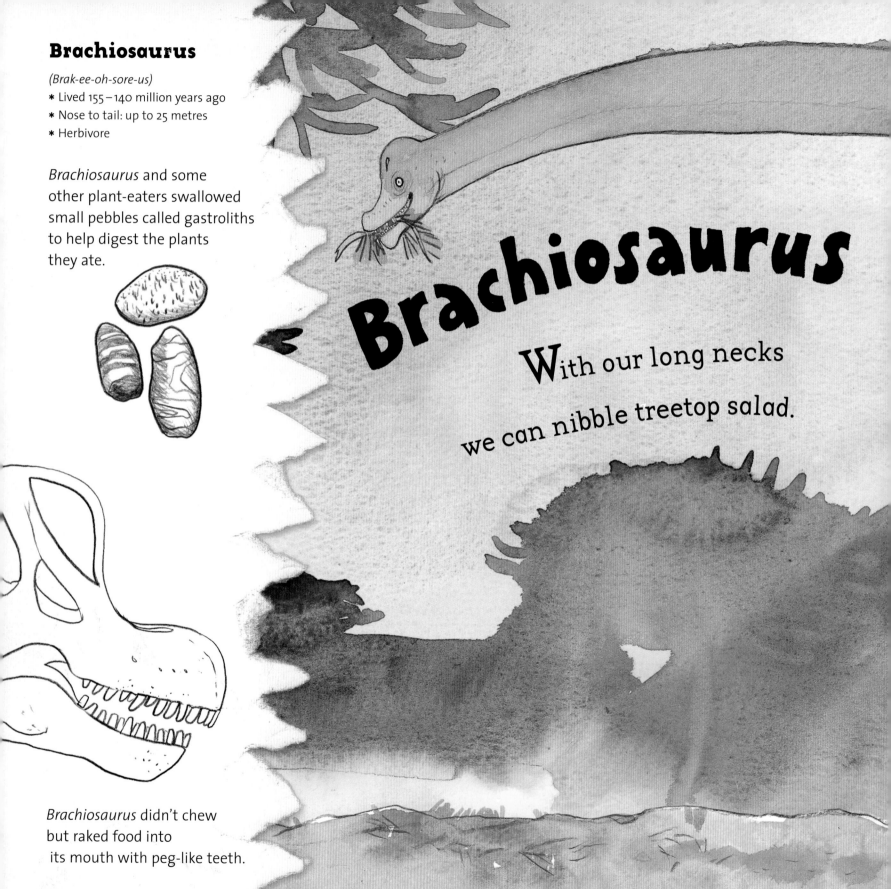

Brachiosaurus

With our long necks

we can nibble treetop salad.

Brachiosaurus didn't chew but raked food into its mouth with peg-like teeth.

It tastes green and fresh with
a tangy flavour of pine nuts.

We rake and swallow.

We don't bother to chew.

But treetop salad always makes us...

POO!

The huge amount of plant material *Brachiosaurus* ate meant that it made enormous poos – rather like giant elephant droppings.

Fossil poos are called coprolites and they tell dinosaur experts a lot about what dinosaurs ate.

Glossary

Cannibal
An animal that eats other animals of its own kind.

Carnivore
An animal that eats only meat.

Coprolites
Fossilised poo that can tell us a lot about what different dinosaurs had for dinner.

Drought
When it doesn't rain for a long time, plants and animals die because they can't find anything to drink or eat.

Fossil
The remains of animals and plants that have been dead and buried for so long that they turn to stone.

Gastroliths
Some plant-eating dinosaurs swallowed pebbles to help them break up the tough plant fibres in their stomachs.

mya = million years ago

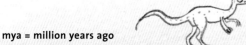

248 mya   Triassic   205 mya

Jurassic

Hadrosaur
The name given to the family of 'duck-billed', plant-eating dinosaurs to which *Edmontosaurus* belonged.

Herbivore
An animal that eats only plants.

Omnivore
An animal that eats both plants and meat.

Predator
An animal that hunts other animals for food.

Prey
An animal that is hunted by other animals for food.

Scales
Small, hard plates that cover fish, reptiles and other animals.

Serrated teeth
Teeth with notches or grooves on their edges that make a good cutting surface, like a knife.

Starvation
When there isn't enough food to eat, animals are so hungry that they start to die.

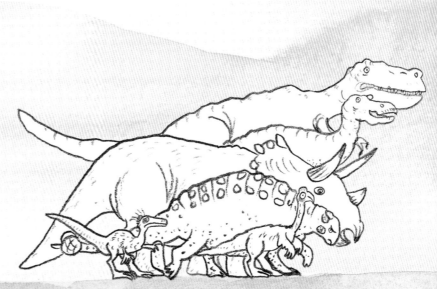

144 mya

Cretaceous

MORE TITLES BY MICK MANNING AND BRITA GRANSTRÖM
FROM FRANCES LINCOLN CHILDREN'S BOOKS

YUCK!

What's for supper?
A wriggly worm? YUCK! Come and join
all sorts of animal babies in the slimiest, stinkiest,
most revolting feast ever. But with spiders, lizards
and rotten eggs on the menu, who will say
YUM and who will say YUCK?

ISBN 10: 1-84507-423-8
ISBN 13: 978-1-84507-423-4

SNAP!

There's a fly buzzing by... SNAP!
Fly is eaten by Frog! Follow the food chain
as each creature is gobbled up by an even larger one.
But which is the biggest animal of all
getting ready to SNAP?

ISBN 10: 1-84507-408-4
ISBN 13: 978-1-84507-408-1

Frances Lincoln titles are available from all good bookshops.
You can also buy books and find out more about your favourite titles,
authors and illustrators on our website: www.franceslincoln.com